THE PRESIDENTS

The PRESI

Edited & Drawn

CROWN PUBLISHERS, INC. ★

DENTS

FROM GEORGE WASHINGTON TO THE PRESENT

in One Line by

OSCAR BERGER

NEW YORK

Books by OSCAR BERGER

TIP AND TOP

AESOP'S FOIBLES

A LA CARTE . . .

FAMOUS FACES

MY VICTIMS

I LOVE YOU . . .

THE PRESIDENTS

LIBRARY OF CONGRESS CATALOG CARD NUMBER: 68-9068

PRINTED IN THE UNITED STATES OF AMERICA

PUBLISHED SIMULTANEOUSLY IN CANADA BY
GENERAL PUBLISHING COMPANY LIMITED

FOREWORD

The Presidents need no introduction. Their lives, deeds, virtues and weaknesses, their words—and even their silences, are our historical heritage, documented and discussed by historians in thousands of volumes running into hundreds of pages each.

This immense library of Americana is a detailed chronology of perils and victories in building a *new* world, with a government "of the people, by the people, for the people": the miracle of the United States of America, growing from an infant rural country into a world power unparalleled in history.

The vast panorama of vital events of nearly two hundred years of history, the drama of great Presidential decisions, affecting the very life and destiny of the Nation and often that of the world, is impossible to capture in a few brief lines of quotations, of course. And if I succeeded in giving a glimpse into the Presidents' characters, wit and wisdom, or occasional lack of it, I achieved my purpose, I think. My unaware co-authors in this attempt are the distinguished company of the thirty-five American Presidents, as the quotations from their words mirror their thoughts and feelings.

My drawings, each President drawn in one line, are a calligraphical exercise. If you draw an imaginary line between each individual drawing, the continuous line becomes symbolic: the Presidency goes on without interruption, despite the astounding variety of Chief Executives. Through the bearded and the clean-jowled, the somber and the sly, the able and the not-so-able, the line flows along, endlessly witnessing the persistence of the American consensus.

Thou, too, sail on, O Ship of State!
Sail on, O Union, strong and great!
Humanity with all its fears,
With all the hopes of future years,
Is hanging breathless on thy fate!

—Henry Wadsworth Longfellow (1807-1882)
"Building of the Ship"

CONTENTS

First Inauguration: April 30, 1789

I do solemnly swear that I will faithfully
execute the office of President of the
United States and will, to the best of my
ability, preserve, protect and defend the
Constitution of the United States.

                       —PRESIDENTIAL OATH

GEORGE WASHINGTON

1732–1799

President: 1789–1797

My movements to the chair of government will be accompanied by feelings not unlike those of a culprit who is going to the place of his execution.

★

Be courteous to all but intimate with few; and let those few be well tried before you give them your confidence.

★

Undertake not what you cannot perform, but be careful to keep your promise.

★

The smiles of heaven can never be expected on a nation that disregards the eternal rules of order and right which heaven itself has ordained.

★

I grieve for the death of our countrymen, but rejoice that the British are still so determined to keep God on our side.

★

To be prepared for war is one of the most effectual means of preserving peace.

★

The basis of our political system is the right of the people to make and to alter their constitution of government.

★

But let there be no change of government by usurpation; for though this, in one instance may be the instrument of good, it is the customary weapon by which free governments are destroyed.

★

Observe good faith and justice towards all nations; cultivate peace and harmony with all.

★

Though, in reviewing incidents of my administration, I am unconscious of intentional errors, I am nevertheless too sensible of my defects not to think it probable that I may have committed many errors.

JOHN ADAMS

1735–1826

President: 1797–1801

There never was a democracy that did not commit suicide.

★

The declaration that our people are hostile to a government made by themselves, for themselves, and conducted by themselves, is an insult.

★

The jaws of power are always open to devour, and her arm is always stretched out, if possible, to destroy the freedom of thinking, speaking and writing.

★

The Bible is the best book in the world. It contains more of my little philosophy than all the libraries I have seen; and such parts of it as I cannot reconcile to my little philosophy, I postpone for future investigation.

★

The question before the human race is, whether the God of Nature shall govern the world by His own laws or whether priests and kings shall rule it by fictious miracles.

★

Or, in other words, whether authority is originally in the people or whether it has descended for 1800 years in a succession of Popes and bishops, or brought down from heaven by the Holy Ghost in the form of a dove, in a phial of holy oil?

★

While all other sciences have advanced, that of government is at a stand; little better understood, little better practised now, than three or four thousand years ago.

★

My opinion against slavery has always been known, and my practice has been so conformable to my sentiments that I have always employed freemen, both as domestics and laborers, and never in my life did I own a slave.

★

Without running a parallel between the President of the United States and the King of England, it is certain that the honor, dignity, and consistency of government is of as much importance to the people in one case as the other.

★

Swim or sink, live or die, survive or perish with my country was my unalterable determination.

John Adams

THOMAS JEFFERSON

1743–1826

President: 1801–1809

Equal rights for all, special privileges for none.

★

A little rebellion, now and then, is a good thing.

★

We hold these truths to be sacred and indeniable; that all men are created equal and independent, that from that equal creation they derive rights inherent and inalienable, among which are the preservation of life, and liberty, and the pursuit of happiness.

★

The execution of the laws is more important than the making of them.

★

The care of human life and happiness, and not their destruction, is the first and only legitimate object of good government.

★

Were it left to me to decide whether we should have a government without newspapers or newspapers without government, I should not hesitate a moment to prefer the latter.

★

I cannot live without books.

★

Enlighten the people generally and tyranny and oppressions of both mind and body will vanish like evil spirits at the dawn of day.

★

I have sworn upon the altar of God eternal hostility against every form of tyranny over the mind of man.

★

No man will ever bring out of the Presidency the reputation which carries him into it.

JAMES MADISON

1751–1836

President: 1809–1817

Every word of the Constitution decides a question between power and liberty.

★

Liberty and order will never be *perfectly* safe, until a trespass on the Constitutional provisions for either, shall be felt with the same keenness that resents an invasion of the dearest rights, until every citizen shall be an Argus to espy, and an Aegeon to avenge, the unhallowed deed.

★

The truth is that all men having power ought to be mistrusted.

★

In Republics the great danger is, that the majority may not sufficiently respect the rights of the minority.

★

The circulation of confidence is better than the circulation of money.

★

A universal and perpetual peace, it is to be feared, is in the catalogue of events, which will never exist but in the imaginations of visionary philosphers, or in the breasts of benevolent enthusiasts.

★

Conscience is the most sacred of all property.

★

Each generation should be made to bear the burden of its own wars instead of carrying them on at the expense of other generations.

★

The ten commandments and the sermon on the Mount contain my religion.

★

If men were angels, no government would be necessary. If angels were to govern men, neither external or internal controls on government would be necessary.

JAMES MONROE

1758–1831

President: 1817–1825

A little flattery will support a man through great fatigue.

★

Surely, if the United States have a right to make war, they have a right to prevent it.

★

Peace is the best time for improvement and preparation of every kind; it is in peace that our commerce flourishes most, that taxes are most easily paid, and that the revenue is most productive.

★

We must support our rights or lose our character, and with it, perhaps, our liberties. A people who fail to do it, can scarcely be said to hold a place among independent nations.

★

. . .The American continents, by the free and independent condition which they have assumed and maintain, are henceforth not to be considered as subjects for future colonization by any European power. . . .

★

We owe it therefore, to candor and to the amicable relations existing between the United States and those powers to declare that we should consider any attempt on their part to extend their system to any portion of this hemisphere as dangerous to our peace and safety.

★

The American people have encountered together great dangers and sustained severe trials with great success.

★

Our population has augmented in an astonishing degree and extended in every direction . . . Louisiana, with a fair and liberal boundary on the western side and the Floridas on the eastern, have been ceded to us. . . .We now comprise within our limits the dimensions and faculties of a great power.

★

I am against every invitation to war, an advocate of peace.

James Monroe

JOHN QUINCY ADAMS

1767–1848

President: 1825–1829

To believe all men honest would be folly. To believe none so is something worse.

★

From the experience of the past we derive instructive lessons for the future.

★

Always vote for a principle, though you vote alone, and you may cherish the sweet reflection that your vote is never lost.

★

If slavery must go by blood and war, let war come.

★

I consider an unjust war as the greatest of all human atrocities, but I esteem a just one as the highest of all human virtues.

★

Let us not be unmindful that liberty is power; that the nation blessed with the largest portion of liberty must in proportion to its numbers be the most powerful nation upon earth.

★

Among the first, perhaps the very first, instrument for the improvement of the condition of men is knowledge.

★

The spirit of improvement is abroad upon the earth.

★

While foreign nations less blessed with that freedom which is power than ourselves are advancing with giant strides in the career of public improvement, were we to slumber in indolence or fold up our arms and proclaim to the world that we are palsied by the will of our constituents, would it not be to cast away the bounties of Providence and doom ourselves to perpetual inferiority?

★

I can never be sure of writing a line that will not some day be published by friend or foe. Nor can I write a sentence suspectible of an odious misconstruction but it will be seized upon and bandied about like a watchword for hatred and derision. This condition of things gives style the cramp.

J. Q. Adams

ANDREW JACKSON

1767–1845

President: 1829–1837

Great is the stake placed in our hands. . . .

Peace, above all things is to be desired, but blood must sometimes be spilled to obtain it on equable and lasting terms.

One man with courage makes a majority.

Heaven will be no heaven to me if I do not meet my wife there.

Events have satisfied my mind, and I think the minds of the American people, that the mischiefs and dangers which flow from a national bank far overflow its advantages.

Shall the rights of the common man be respected or shall the rich rule the country again?

If the Government would confine itself to equal protection, and, as Heaven does its rains, showers its favors alike on the high and the low, the rich and the poor, it would be an unqualified blessing.

Our Union: it must be preserved! Without union our Independence would never have been achieved. Without union they never can be maintained.

As long as our Government is administered for the good of the people, and is regulated by their will . . . it will be worth defending.

I have accustomed myself to receive with respect the opinions of others, but always take the responsibility of deciding for myself.

MARTIN VAN BUREN

1782–1862

President: 1837–1841

From a small community we have risen to a people powerful in numbers and in strength.

★

America will present to every friend of mankind the cheering proof that a popular government, wisely formed, is wanting in no element of endurance and strength. Fifty years ago its rapid failure was boldly predicted.

★

Free and unbiased exercise of political opinion is the only sure foundation and safe-guard of republican government.

★

There is a power in public opinion in this country—and I thank God for it; for it is the most honest and best of all powers—which will not tolerate an incompetent or unworthy man to hold in his weak or wicked hands the lives and fortunes of his fellow citizens. This power operates alike upon the government and the incumbent.

★

The less government interferes with private pursuits the better for the general prosperity.

★

Indebtedness can not be lessened by borrowing more money, or by changing the form of the debt.

★

It is only by retrenchment and reform—by curtailing public and private expenditures, by paying our debts, and by reforming our banking system—that we are to expect effectual relief, security for the future, and an enduring prosperity.

★

In the shock of contending empires it is only by assuming a resolute bearing and clothing themselves with defensive armor that neutral nations can maintain their independent rights.

★

The President under our system, like the King in a monarchy, never dies.

WILLIAM HENRY HARRISON

1773–1841

President: 1841

It is cheaper to feed the Indians than to fight them.

★

I think I have personally obtained for the country from the Indians many more millions of acres of land than the sword of a conqueror ever permanently won.

★

Every citizen a soldier. . . . The whole secret of ancient military glory will be found in the military education of the youth.

★

Power is insinuating. Few men are satisfied with less power than they are able to procure. No lover is ever satisfied with the first smile of his mistress.

★

See that the Government does not acquire too much power. Keep a check upon your rulers. Do this and liberty is safe.

★

I am and ever have been a Democratic Republican. Being a child of the revolution and bred in its principles, I believe in the right and ability of the people to govern themselves.

★

I am the most persecuted and calumniated individual now living; because I have been slandered by reckless opponents to the extent that I am devoid of every qualification, physical, mental and moral, for the high place to which at least a respectable portion of my fellow citizens have nominated me.

★

A decent and manly examination of the acts of Government should be not only tolerated, but encouraged.

JOHN TYLER

1790–1862

President: 1841–1845

All is wisely ordered by Providence.

★

The barking of newspapers and the brawling of demagogues can never drive me from my course.

★

It is true that the succession of the Vice-President to the Chief Magistracy has never occurred before and that all prudent and patriotic minds have looked on this new trial of the wisdom and stability of our institutions with a somewhat anxious concern.

★

I have been made to feel too sensibly the difficulties of my unprecedented position not to know all that is intended to be conveyed in the reproach cast upon a President without a party.

★

I felt that a high and solemn duty had devolved upon me . . . I considered the path of my duty was clearly marked out before me, and I resolved to pursue it.

★

For having declined of late to unite in giving away a fruitful source of revenue, from a Treasury which has become nearly exhausted, I have been charged with a desire to dictate to Congress, when my sole object is to carry out a law of this very Congress on the subject of public lands.

★

The Constitution never designed that the executive should be a mere cipher. On the contrary, it denies to Congress the right to pass any law without his approval.

★

If the annexation of Texas shall crown off my public life, I shall neither retire ignominiously nor be soon forgotten.

JAMES KNOX POLK

1795–1849

President: 1845–1849

We have a country as well as a party to obey.

★

No President who performs his duty faithfully and conscientiously can have any leisure.

★

I prefer to supervise the whole operations of the Government myself rather than entrust the public business to subordinates, and this makes my duties very great.

★

In the act of declaring war [against Mexico] Congress provided raising men and money to enable the President "to prosecute it to a speedy and successful termination."

★

I am held responsible for the conduct of the war, and yet Congress refused to give me a commander in whom I have confidence, and I am compelled to employ the officers whom the law has provided, however unfit they may be.

★

None can fail to see the danger to our safety and future peace if Texas remains an independent state or becomes an ally or dependency of some foreign nation more powerful than herself.

★

The blessings of Liberty which our Constitution secures may be enjoyed alike by minorities and majorities.

★

Equal and exact justice should characterize all our intercourse with foreign countries.

★

With me it is emphatically true that the Presidency is "no bed of roses."

ZACHARY TAYLOR

1784–1850

President: 1849–1850

My life has been devoted to arms, yet I look upon war, at all times . . . as a national calamity, to be avoided if compatible with the national honor.

★

I have no private purpose to accomplish, no party projects to build up, no enemies to punish, nothing to serve but my Country . . . I shall engage in no schemes, no combinations, no intrigues.

★

I shall make honesty, capacity and fidelity indispensable prerequisites to the disposal of office, and the absence of [any] of these qualities shall be deemed sufficient cause for removal.

★

The United States bank "is dead" and will not be revived in my lifetime.

★

I will not make myself unhappy at what I cannot prevent, nor give up the Constitution or abandon it because a rent has been made in it, but will stick by and repair it, and nurse it as long as it will hang together.

★

Stand firm, don't yield, it means disunion and I am pained to learn that we have disunion men to deal with; disunion is treason.

★

For more than half a century, during which kingdoms and empires have fallen, this Union has stood unshaken.

★

I did not think it wise or just, to kick away the ladder by which I ascended to the Presidency; colonels, majors, captains, lieutenants, sergeants, and corporals are just as necessary to success in politics as they are to discipline and efficiency in an army.

★

Rotation in office, provided good men are appointed, is sound republican doctrine.

Zachary Taylor

MILLARD FILLMORE

1800–1874

President: 1850–1853

The man who can look upon a crisis without being willing to offer himself upon the altar of his country is not fit for public trust.

★

God knows that I detest slavery, but it is an existing evil, for which we are not responsible, and we must endure it and give it such protection as is guaranteed by the Constitution, till we can get rid of it without destroying the last hope of free government in the world.

★

Church and state should be separate, not only in form, but fact—religion and politics should not be mingled.

★

I have no hostility to foreigners. I trust I am their friend.

★

I rejoice in all measures which extend and increase our means of intercourse with foreign countries, and strengthen and enlarge our foreign commerce.

★

The law is the only sure protection of the weak, and the only efficient restraint upon the strong.

★

Without law there can be no real practical liberty, that when the law is trampled under foot tyranny rules, whether it appears in the form of a military despotism or of popular violence.

★

Before lasting peace can be restored, much must be forgiven, if not forgotten.

★

I am tolerant of all creeds. Yet if any sect suffered itself to be used for political objects, I would meet it by political opposition.

★

We elect a man to the Presidency, expect him to be honest, to give up a lucrative profession, perhaps, and after we have done with him, we let him go into seclusion and perhaps poverty.

FRANKLIN PIERCE

1804–1869

President: 1853–1857

I acknowledge my obligations to the masses of my countrymen, and to them alone.

★

If a man who has attained this high office cannot free himself from cliques and act independently, our Constitution is valueless.

★

While men inhabiting different parts of this vast continent cannot be expected to hold the same opinions . . . they can unite in a common object and sustain common principles essential to the maintenance of that object.

★

Political services and personal friendship furnish no claim to office.

★

We have nothing in our history or position to invite aggression; we have everything to beckon us to the cultivation of relations of peace and amity with all nations.

★

Long experience has shown that, in general, when the principal powers of Europe are engaged in war, the rights of neutral nations are endangered.

★

My doctrine is that almost everything depends upon ourselves.

★

No citizen of our country should permit himself to forget that he is part of its Government and entitled to be heard in the determination of its policy and its measures, and that therefore the highest considerations of personal honor and patriotism require him to maintain by whatever of power or influence he may possess the integrity of the laws of the Republic.

★

I cannot find any authority in the Constitution for making the Federal Government the great almoner of public charity throughout the United States. . . .

JAMES BUCHANAN

1791–1868

President: 1857–1861

My principles are convictions.

★

Self-preservation is the first instinct of nature, and therefore any state of society in which the sword is all the time suspended over the heads of the people must at last become intolerable.

★

We ought to do justice in a kindly spirit to all nations and require justice from them in return.

★

The slavery question, like everything human, will have its day . . . but if in the midst of the existing excitement the Union shall perish, the evil may then become irreparable.

★

There is nothing as stable but Heaven and the Constitution.

★

In Heaven's name, let the trial be made before we plunge into armed conflict. . . . Time is a great conservative power. . . . Disunion ought to be the last desperate remedy of a despairing people. . . .

★

All the friends I loved and wanted to reward are dead and all the enemies I hated and had marked for punishment are turned my friends.

★

I have no other object of earthly ambition than to leave my country in a peaceful and prosperous condition, and to live in the affections and respect of my countrymen.

★

When I parted from President Lincoln, on introducing him to the Executive Mansion, according to custom, I said to him: "If you are as happy, my dear Sir, on entering this house, as I am in leaving it, you are the happiest man in the country!"

James Buchanan

ABRAHAM LINCOLN

1809–1865

President: 1861–1865

Nobody has ever expected me to be President. In my poor lean, lank face, nobody has ever seen that any cabbages were sprouting out.

★

You can fool some of the people all of the time, and all of the people some of the time, but you cannot fool all of the people all of the time.

★

The ballot is stronger than the bullet.

★

No man is good enough to govern another man without that other's consent.

★

I believe this government cannot endure permanently, half slave and half free.

★

Fourscore and seven years ago our fathers brought forth on this continent a new nation, conceived in liberty, and dedicated to the proposition that all men are created equal.

★

With malice toward none; with charity for all; with firmness in the right, as God gives us to see the right, let us strive on to finish the work we are in; to bind up the nation's wounds; to care for him who shall have borne the battle, and for his widow and his orphan—to do all which may achieve and cherish a just and lasting peace among ourselves and with all nations.

★

If I am killed, I can die but once; but to live in constant dread of it, is to die over and over again.

★

I claim not to have controlled events, but confess plainly that events have controlled me.

★

In God's name! If any one can do better in my place than I have done, or am endeavoring to do, let him try his hand at it, and no one will be better contented than myself.

ANDREW JOHNSON

1808–1875

President: 1865–1869

I do not intend to be bullied by my enemies nor overawed by my friends.

★

I am one of those who believe that a man may sin and do wrong, and after that may do right. If all of us who have sinned were put to death—there would not be many of us left.

★

. . . Taxes should be so distributed as not to fall unduly on the poor, but rather on the accumulated wealth of the country.

★

Honest conviction is my courage, the Constitution is my guide.

★

And I say here tonight that if my predecessor had lived, the vials of wrath would have poured out upon him.

★

Away with slavery, the breeder of aristocrats. Up with the Stars and Stripes, symbol of free labor and free men.

★

In the support and practice of correct principles we can never reach wrong results.

★

Gentlemen of the Cabinet: You no doubt are aware that certain evil-disposed persons have formed a conspiracy to depose the President of the United States, and to supply his place by an individual of their own selection.

★

Their plan of operations seems to contemplate certain accusations against the President, which are to take the form of Articles of Impeachment, and that hereupon, before hearing or trial, he is, under color of law, to be placed under arrest, and suspended or removed from office.

★

Men may talk about beheading and about usurpation, but when I am beheaded I want the American people to be witnesses.

ULYSSES S. GRANT

1822–1885

President: 1869–1877

Let us have peace.

A military life had no charms for me . . . I was fond of agriculture, and of all employment in which horses were used.

The civil war was a fearful lesson, and should teach us the necessity of avoiding wars in the future.

The effects of the late civil war have been to free the slave and make him a citizen. Yet he is not possessed of the civil rights which citizenship should carry with it. This is wrong and should be corrected.

It was my fortune, or misfortune, to be called to the office of Chief Executive without any previous political training. Under such circumstances it is but reasonable to suppose that errors of judgment must have occurred.

History shows that no administration from the time of Washington to the present has been free from these mistakes. But I leave comparisons to history, claiming only that I have acted in every instance from a conscientious desire to do what was right, constitutional, within the law, and for the very best interests of the whole people.

God gave us Lincoln and Liberty, let us fight for both.

Keep the church and the State for ever separate.

★

I believe that our Great Maker is preparing the world in His own good time to become one nation, speaking one language, when armies and navies will no longer be required.

★

I know only two tunes, one of them is "Yankee Doodle," and the other isn't.

RUTHERFORD B. HAYES

1822–1893

President: 1877–1881

He serves his party best who serves his country best.

★

No person connected with me by blood or marriage will be appointed to office.

★

My policy is trust peace, and put aside the bayonet.

★

On the Temperance question: it seemed to me that the example of excluding liquors from the White House would be wise and useful and would be approved by good people generally. I knew it would be particularly gratifying to Mrs. Hayes to have done it.

★

Strikers prevent men willing to work from doing so. Every man has a right to refuse to work if the wages don't suit him, but no man has a right to prevent others from working.

★

If clouds cast their shadows on your path, we are cheered also by the sunlight of prosperity.

★

No misconduct of any sort—no corruption in office is covered up by the Administration. All officers understand that a betrayal of trust will lead to speedy, unsparing and thorough prosecution and punishment.

★

I am not liked as a President by the politicians in office, in the press, or in Congress. But I am content to abide by the judgment—the sober second thought—of the people.

★

Presidents in the past have always been better than their adversaries have predicted. All were free from the taint of personal corruption. All were honest men.

★

Looking back on my administration, I can say with truth: I left this great country prosperous and happy, and the party of my choice strong, victorious and united.

JAMES A. GARFIELD

1831–1881

President: 1881

It better be known in the outset whether the President is the head of the Government, or the registering clerk of the Senate.

★

I would rather be beaten in Right than succeed in Wrong.

★

A law is not a law without coercion behind it.

★

Once or twice I felt like crying out in the agony of my soul against the greed for office and its consumption of my time. My services ought to be worth more to the government than to be spent thus. . . . It will cost me some struggle to keep from despising the office seeker.

★

All free governments are managed by the combined wisdom and folly of the people.

★

Next in importance to freedom and justice is popular education, without which neither freedom nor justice can be permanently maintained.

★

This nation must open up new avenues of work and usefulness to the women of this country.

★

Ideas are the great warriors of the world, and a war which has no ideas behind it, is simply a brutality.

★

Some Civil Service Reform will come by necessity after the wearisome years of wasted Presidents have paved the way for it.

★

I do not care what others say or think about me. But there is one man's opinion which I very much value, and that is the opinion of James Garfield.

CHESTER ALAN ARTHUR

1830-1886

President: 1881-1885

Men may die, but the fabrics of our free institutions remain unshaken.

★

No higher proof could exist of the strength of popular government than the fact that, though the chosen of the people be struck down, his constitutional successor is peacefully installed without shock or strain.

★

As the long peace that has lulled us into a sense of fancied security may at any time be disturbed, it is plain that the policy of strengthening our Navy is dictated by considerations of wise economy, of just regard for our future tranquillity, and of true appreciation of the dignity and honor of the Republic.

★

The opening of China to the commerce of the whole world has benefited no section more than the States of our own Pacific Coast.

★

Experience has shown that the trade of the East is the key to national wealth and influence.

★

Now you were never more mistaken in your life than to suppose that the business men carry elections. A large vote is brought out when all the men in politics are pleased and satisfied and set to work with enthusiasm for the ticket.

★

They bring out the votes, and if you trusted these elections to business men and merely respectable influences, the Democratic Party would get in every time (by default).

★

Our long-established friendliness with Russia has remained unshaken. It has prompted me to proffer the earnest counsels of this Government that measures be adopted for suppressing the proscription which the Hebrew race in that country has lately suffered.

★

There is reason to believe that the time is not far distant when Russia will be able to secure toleration to all faiths within her borders.

★

A nation is justified in repudiating its treaty obligations only when they are in conflict with great paramount interests.

GROVER CLEVELAND

1837–1908

President: 1885–1889 and 1893–1897

Men and times change—but principles—never.

★

Gentlemen, I will not go into the White House pledged to you or anyone else. I will make no secret promises. I'll be damned if I will.

★

Patriotism is no substitute for a sound currency.

★

Contented labor is an element of national prosperity.

★

Every citizen owes to the country a vigilant watch and close scrutiny of its public servants and a fair and reasonable estimate of their fidelity and usefulness.

★

What is the use of being elected or reelected, unless you stand for something?

★

I am President of all the people, good, bad, or indifferent, and as long as my opinions are known, ought perhaps to keep myself out of their squabbles.

★

Under our scheme of Government the waste of public money is a crime against the citizen.

★

To secure the fitness and competency of appointees to office and remove from political action the demoralizing madness for spoils, civil-service reform has found a place in our public policy and laws.

★

I go to bed after a long day with the feeling that I must be the meanest man in the world, for I seem to say only "no" where I would be only too glad to say "yes." But this Office-seeking is a disease.—I am entirely satisfied of that!

BENJAMIN HARRISON

1833–1901

President: 1889–1893

No Harrison has ever retreated in the presence of a foe without giving battle, and so I have determined to stand and fight.

★

I want it understood that I am the grandson of nobody. I believe that every man should stand on his own merits.

★

The man who has come to regard the ballot box as a juggler's hat has renounced his allegiance.

★

Laws do not execute themselves. Somebody must look after them. It is the duty of the President to see that every law passed by Congress is executed.

★

The newspapers must not be taken too seriously.

★

Honorable party service will certainly not be esteemed by me a disqualification for public office, but it will in no case be allowed to serve as a shield of official negligence, incompetency or delinquency.

★

We Americans have no commission from God to police the world.

★

If our great corporations would more scrupulously observe their legal limitations and duties, they would have less cause to complain of the unlawful limitations of their rights or of violent interference with their operations.

★

Passion has swept some of our communities, but only to give us a new demonstration that the great body of our people are stable, patriotic and law-abiding.

★

Great lives do not go out. They go on.

WILLIAM McKINLEY

1843–1901

President: 1897–1901

The free man cannot be long an ignorant man.

★

Let us ever remember that our interest is in concord not in conflict and our real eminence as a nation lies in the victories of peace, not those of war.

★

When we go to war it will be for humanity's sake.

★

For labor a short day is better than a short dollar.

★

God and man have linked the nations together. No nation can longer be indifferent to any other. The period of exclusiveness is past.

★

And as we are brought more and more in touch with each other, the less occasion there is for misunderstandings and the stronger the disposition, when we have differences, to adjust them in the court of arbitration, which is the noblest forum for settlement of international differences.

★

I can no longer be called the President of a party; I am the President of the whole people.

★

Half-heartedness never won a battle.

★

Liberty to make our laws does not give us license to break them.

★

Business life, whether among ourselves or with other people, is ever a sharp struggle for success. It will be none the less so in the future. Without competition we would be clinging to the clumsy antiquated processes of farming and manufacture and the methods of business of long ago, and the twentieth would be no further advanced than the eighteenth century. But though commercial competitors we are, commercial enemies we must not be.

THEODORE ROOSEVELT

1858–1919

President: 1901–1909

Life is a great adventure.

★

The government is us; we are the government, you and I.

★

I took the Canal Zone and let Congress debate, and while the debate goes on the Canal does also.

★

The only safe rule is to promise little and faithfully to keep every promise, to "speak softly and carry a big stick."

★

We demand that big business give people a square deal, in return we must insist that when anyone engaged in big business honestly endeavors to do right, he shall himself be given a square deal.

★

A great democracy must be progressive or it soon ceases to be a great democracy.

★

The nation behaves well if it treats the natural resources as assets which it must turn over to the next generation increased, and not impaired in value.

★

History would be worse than useless if it doesn't tell the exact truth, and if it doesn't tell of our disasters and shortcomings as well as our triumphs.

★

Much has been given us, and much will rightfully be expected from us. We have duties to others and duties to ourselves. We have become a great nation. . . .

★

No President ever enjoyed himself in the Presidency as much as I did.

Theodore Roosevelt

WILLIAM HOWARD TAFT

1857–1930

President: 1909–1913

The administration of justice lies at the foundation of Government.

★

I love judges and I love courts. They are my ideals, that typify on earth what we shall meet hereafter in heaven under a just God.

★

Wealth used as capital is the basis of modern civilization, that the right of property is the most valuable right in building up our society next to the right of personal liberty.

★

"War is Hell," as one of our great generals has said, and nothing but a great and unavoidable cause can justify it.

★

Our international policy is always to promote peace.

★

I am not in favor of suffrage for women until I can be convinced that all women desire it; and when they desire it I am in favor of giving it to them.

★

Antisemitism is a noxious weed that should be cut out. It has no place in America.

★

I hate to use the patronage as a club unless I have to.

★

I am afraid I am a constant disappointment to my party. The fact of the matter is, the longer I am President, the less of a party man I seem to become . . . it seems to me to be impossible to be a strict party man and serve the whole country impartially.

★

One cannot always be sure of the truth of what one hears if he happens to be the President of the United States.

WOODROW WILSON

1856–1924

President: 1913–1921

America cannot be an ostrich with its head in the sand. America cannot shut itself out from the rest of the world.

★

One cool judgment is worth a thousand hasty councils. The thing to do is to supply light and not heat.

★

The world must be made safe for democracy.

★

Conservatism is the policy of "make no change and consult your grandmother when in doubt."

★

What difference does party make when mankind is involved?

★

If you want to make enemies, try to change something.

★

Militarism does not consist in the existence of any army. . . . Militarism is a spirit. It is a point of view. It is a system. It is a purpose. The purpose of militarism is to use armies for aggression.

★

Only a peace between equals can last. Only a peace the very principle of which is equality and a common participation in a common benefit. . . . I am proposing that no nation should seek to extend its polity over any other nation or people, but that every people should be left free to determine its own polity, its own way of developing unhindered, unthreatened, unafraid, the little along with the great and powerful.

★

The League of Nations was the only hope for mankind. . . . Dare we reject it and break the heart of the world?

★

I can predict with absolute certainty that within another generation there will be another world war if the nations of the world do not concert the method by which to prevent it.

WARREN G. HARDING

1865–1923

President: 1921–1923

In this job I am not worried about my enemies. I can take care of them. It is my friends who are giving me trouble.

★

I listen to one side and they seem right, and then . . . I talk to the other side and they seem just as right, and there I am where I started! God, what a job!

★

If revolution insists upon overturning established order, let other people make the tragic experiment. There is no place for it in America.

★

We want a period in America with less Government in business and more business in Government.

★

War made us a creditor nation. We did not seek an excess possession of the world's gold. . . . We do not seek to become an international dictator because of its power.

★

Whether the League of Nations achieves the great things hoped for, or comes to supersedure, or to failure, the American unwillingness to be part of it has been expressed.

★

I stand against an association of nations in which we will be under the flag of a world super-government, and no longer under the American flag. To serve mankind it is not necessary to subject one country to foreclosure by the sheriff of internationalism.

★

America's present need is not heroics but healing; not nostrums but normalcy; not revolution but restoration; not surgery but serenity.

★

Understanding—that is what the world and the nation most need.

★

The White House is a prison. I can't get away from the men who dog my footsteps. I am in jail.

64

CALVIN COOLIDGE

1872–1933

President: 1923–1929

No one knows how I hate making speeches.

★

The fundamental precept of liberty is toleration.

★

Character is the only secure foundation of the State.

★

Borrowed money, even when owing to a nation by another nation, should be repaid.

★

We want wealth, but there are many other things we want very much more. Among them are peace, honor, charity and idealism.

★

Economy is idealism in its most practical form.

★

If people want to fight, they'll fight with broomsticks if they can't find anything else.

★

We are against war because it is destructive. We are for peace because it is constructive.

★

War is the rule of force. Peace is the reign of law. Let war and all force end, and peace and all law reign.

★

It is not necessary to suppose that our civilization is perfect.

HERBERT HOOVER

1874–1964

President: 1929–1933

Food will win the war.

★

Words are not of any great importance in times of economic disturbance. It is action that counts.

★

One who brandishes a pistol must be prepared to shoot.

★

To maintain peace is as dynamic in its requirements as the conduct of war. We can not say "Let there be peace" and go about other business.

★

The obvious way to lessen the losses and miseries of depression is first to check the destructive extremes of booms. Mitigation of depression is a further task of relief and reconstruction.

★

...The great causes of world peace, world disarmament and world recovery must prevail. They cannot prevail until a path to their attainment is built upon honest friendship, mutual confidence, and proper co-operation among nations.

★

As a nation we must prevent hunger and cold to those of our people who are in honest difficulties.

★

Fishing is the only labor or recreation open to a President in which both the press and the public are prepared to concede privacy.

★

No man could be President without looking back upon the effort given to the country by the thirty Presidents who in my case have preceded me. No man of imagination can be President without thinking of what shall be the course of his country under the thirty more Presidents who will follow him. He must think of himself as a link in the long chain of his country's destiny, past and future.

★

Older men declare war. But it is youth that must fight and die.

FRANKLIN D. ROOSEVELT

1882–1945

President: 1933–1945

I pledge you, I pledge myself, to a new deal for the American people.

★

This generation of Americans has a rendezvous with destiny.

★

The only thing we have to fear is fear itself.

★

A Government can be no better than the public opinion which sustains it.

★

In the face of great perils never before encountered, our strong purpose is to protect and to perpetuate the integrity of democracy.

★

We must be the great arsenal of democracy.

★

In the future days, which we seek to make secure, we look forward to a world founded upon four essential human freedoms: The first is freedom of speech and expression—everywhere in the world. The second is freedom of every person to worship God in his own way, everywhere in the world. The third is freedom from want—everywhere in the world. The fourth is freedom from fear—anywhere in the world.

★

If the human race as a whole is to survive, the world must find the way by which men and nations can live together in peace. We cannot accept the doctrine that war must be forever a part of man's destiny.

★

I cannot go any faster than the public will let me.

★

At night, when I lay my head on my pillow . . . and I think of the things that had come before me during the day, and the decisions I have made, I say to myself—well, I have done the best I could—and I turn over and go to sleep.

Franklin D Roosevelt

HARRY S. TRUMAN

1884–

President: 1945–1953

In performing the duties of my office, I need the help and prayers of every one of you, I ask for your encouragement and your support.

★

The fact that we can release atomic energy ushers in a new era of man's understanding of nature's forces. Atomic energy may in the future supplement the power that now comes from coal, oil and water.

★

We must harness this great energy source of nature unlocked by man for the benefit and not the destruction of man. Today it helps protect us, tomorrow it will also serve us.

★

Another world war would put civilization back some thousand years or more.

★

I consider the Point Four program the most important peace policy development of my administration. Briefly stated, Point Four is a proposition to take over the gap that is left by the failure of colonialism in that its objective is to help people to help themselves.

★

We have bought time at great expense and a terrible cost of lives and fortune and now we must use that time intelligently and courageously.

★

The Truman Doctrine, the Marshall Plan, the North Atlantic Pact, the mobilization program and the action by the United Nations in meeting the military aggression in Korea were steps dictated by a series of emergencies.

★

I missed being a musician and the real and only reason I missed being one is because I wasn't good enough.

★

I shall continue to do what I think is right whether anybody likes it or not.

★

It is much better to go down fighting for what is right than to compromise your principles.

DWIGHT D. EISENHOWER

1890–

President: 1953–1961

Morale is the greatest single factor in successful wars.

★

A vital element in keeping the peace is our military establishment. Our arms must be mighty, ready for instant action, so that no potential aggressor may be tempted to risk his own destruction.

★

People want peace so much that governments had better get out of their way and let them have it.

★

I hate war as only a soldier who has lived it can, only as one who has seen its brutality, its futility, its stupidity. Yet there is one thing to say on its credit side—victory required mighty manifestation of the most ennobling of virtues of man—faith, courage, fortitude, sacrifice!

★

Only Americans can hurt America.

★

Until war is eliminated from international relations, unpreparedness for it is well-nigh as criminal as war itself.

★

Dollars and guns are no substitute for brains and willpower.

★

I do not believe that any individual whether he is running General Motors or the United States of America, his phase of it, can do the best job by sitting at a desk and putting his face in a bunch of paper.

★

Against the dark background of the atomic bomb, the United States does not wish merely to present strength, but also the desire and hope for peace.

★

No President can delegate his constitutional duties. How can he do it? He has to sign the papers. He has to sign them, and he is responsible for them.

JOHN F. KENNEDY

1917–1963

President: 1961–1963

It is much easier to make the speeches than to make the judgments.

★

We stand today on the edge of a new frontier, a frontier of unknown opportunities and perils, a frontier of unfulfilled hopes and threats.

★

You can always survive a mistake in domestic affairs, but you may get killed by one made in foreign policy.

★

When power leads man toward arrogance, poetry reminds him of his limitations.

★

My fellow Americans: ask not what your country can do for you: Ask what you can do for your country.

★

My fellow citizens of the world: Ask not what America will do for you, but what together we can do for the freedom of man.

★

Let every nation know, whether it wishes us well or ill, that we shall pay any price, bear any burden, meet any hardship, support any friend, oppose any foe to assure the survival and success of liberty.

★

Let both sides to invoke the wonders of science instead of its terrors. Together let us explore the stars, conquer the deserts, eradicate disease, tap the ocean depths, and encourage the arts and commerce.

★

What kind of peace we seek? Not the peace of the grave or the security of the slave. I am talking about genuine peace, the kind of peace that makes life on earth worth living.

★

Mankind must put an end to war—or war will put an end to mankind.

LYNDON B. JOHNSON

1908–

President: 1963–

Come now, and let us reason together . . .

★

Education, more than any single force, will mold the citizen of the future. The classroom—not the trench—is the frontier of freedom. . . .

★

And this administration here and now, declares unconditional war on poverty. Our objective is total victory.

★

Words wound. But as a veteran of twelve years in the United States Senate, I happily attest that they do not kill.

★

We have the opportunity to move, not only toward the rich society and the powerful society, but upward to the Great Society. It rests on abundance and liberty for all. It demands an end to poverty and racial injustice.

★

First—let there be no mistake about it—the looting, arson, plunder and pillage which have occurred are not part of a civil rights protest. There is no American right to loot stores, to burn buildings, to fire rifles from the rooftops. This is crime—and crime must be dealt with forcefully, swiftly, certainly—under law.

★

Peace, an honorable peace, must sometimes be bought at a price. . . .

★

I believe that a peaceful Asia is far nearer to reality because of what America has done in Vietnam.

★

Let us pray that the tide has turned . . . and that future generations will mark 1968 as the year the world turned for all time away from the horrors of war and constructed new bulwarks to peace.

★

. . . I have concluded, that I should not permit the Presidency to become involved in the partisan divisions that are developing in this political year. . . . Accordingly, I shall not seek, and I will not accept, the nomination of my party for another term as your President.

CHRONOLOGY

1.

GEORGE WASHINGTON
1732–1799

1732	Born: February 22, at Wakefield, Westmoreland County, Virginia.
1749	Official surveyor of Culpeper County.
1752	Adjutant General of Virginia militia. Inherited Mount Vernon.
1753	Sent to the Ohio Valley as a militia major, on a winter mission.
1755	Served on the staff of General Braddock.
1759	Married: Martha Dandridge Custis, a widow of twenty-seven (1732–1802).
1759–74	Member House of Burgesses.
1774–75	Member Continental Congress.
1775–83	Commander-in-Chief of the Continental Army.
1781	Accepted the surrender of Cornwallis at Yorktown.
1787	Chairman of the Constitutional Convention.
1789–97	President (Vice-President: John Adams).
1797	Retired to Mount Vernon.
1799	Died: at Mount Vernon, December 14.

2.

JOHN ADAMS
1735–1826

1735	Born: October 30, at Braintree, Massachusetts.
1755	Graduated from Harvard.
1755–58	Taught school.
1758	Admitted to the bar.
1764	Married: Abigail Smith (1744–1818).
1770	Defended British soldiers who fired on civilians in the Boston Massacre.
1774–77	Member of the Continental Congress.
1778–79	Diplomatic missions to France.
1785	Minister to England.
1789	Elected Vice-President.
1792	Reelected Vice-President.
1797–1801	President (Vice-President: Thomas Jefferson).
1800	Moved from Philadelphia to Washington (first occupant of White House).
1826	Died: at Braintree, July 4.

3.

THOMAS JEFFERSON
1743–1826

1743	Born: April 13, at Shadwell, Virginia.
1762	Graduated from College of William and Mary.
1767	Admitted to the bar.
1767	Married: Martha Wayles Skelton (1748–1782).
1769	Elected to the House of Burgesses.
1775–76	Member of the second Continental Congress.
1776	Elected to the Virginia House of Delegates.
1779–81	Governor of Virginia.
1783–85	Member United States Congress.
1785–89	Minister to France.
1790–93	Secretary of State.
1797–1801	Vice-President.
1801–09	President (Vice-Presidents: Aaron Burr, George Clinton).
1809	Retired to Monticello.
1826	Died: July 4, at Monticello, Virginia.

4.

JAMES MADISON
1751–1836

1751	Born: March 16, at Port Conway, Virginia.
1771	Graduated from Princeton.
1776	Member Virginia Assembly.
1780–83	Member Continental Congress.
1787	Member Constitutional Convention.
1789–97	Member United States Congress.
1794	Married: Dolley Payne Todd (1768–1849).
1801–09	Secretary of State.
1809–17	President (Vice-Presidents: George Clinton, Elbridge Gerry).
1826–36	Rector, University of Virginia.
1829	Delegate to the Virginia Constitutional Convention.
1836	Died: June 28, at Montpelier, Virginia.

5.

JAMES MONROE
1758–1831

1758	Born: April 28, in Westmoreland County, Virginia.

1776	Graduated College of William and Mary.
1776	Enlisted Continental Army.
1782	Elected to Virginia Assembly.
1786	Married: Elizabeth Kortright (1768–1830).
1786–90	Practiced law, at Fredericksburg, Virginia.
1790–94	United States Senator.
1794–96	Minister to France.
1799–1802	Governor of Virginia.
1803–07	Minister to England.
1811	Governor of Virginia.
1811–17	Secretary of State (and Secretary of War, 1814–15).
1817–25	President (Vice-President: Daniel D. Tompkins).
1831	Died: July 4, in New York City.

6.

JOHN QUINCY ADAMS

1767–1848

1767	Born: July 11, in Braintree (Quincy), Massachusetts.
1781–83	Secretary to Francis Dana, Minister to Russia.
1788	Graduated from Harvard.
1791	Admitted to the bar.
1794	Minister to the Netherlands.
1797	Married: Louisa Catherine Johnson (1775–1852).
1797–1801	Minister to Berlin.
1803–08	United States Senator.
1809–11	Minister to Russia.
1814	Negotiated peace with England (Treaty of Ghent).
1815–17	Minister to England.
1817–25	Secretary of State.
1825–29	President (Vice-President: John C. Calhoun).
1831–48	Member of Congress.
1848	Died: February 23, in Washington, D.C.

7.

ANDREW JACKSON

1767–1845

1767	Born: March 15, at Waxhaw, South Carolina.
1780–81	Took part and served as messenger in Revolution.
1784	Started the study of law.
1787	Admitted to the bar.
1788	Moved to Nashville, Tennessee to practice law.
1791	Married: Rachel Donelson Robard (1767–1828).
1796	Elected Member of Congress.
1797–98	United States Senator.
1798–1804	Justice of Tennessee Supreme Court.
1801	Became a Major General of Tennessee militia.

1806–12	Lived as prosperous planter.
1812–15	Served in War of 1812.
1817	Conducted Seminole War in Florida.
1821	Governor of Florida.
1823	United States Senator.
1829–37	President (Vice-Presidents: John C. Calhoun, Martin Van Buren).
1845	Died: June 8, at The Hermitage, near Nashville, Tennessee.

8.

MARTIN VAN BUREN

1782–1862

1782	Born: December 5, at Kinderhook, New York.
1803	Admitted to the bar.
1807	Married: Hannah Hoes (1783–1819).
1813–15	New York State Senator.
1816	Attorney General of New York State.
1821–29	United States Senator.
1829	Governor of New York.
1829–31	Secretary of State.
1831–32	Minister to England.
1833–37	Vice-President.
1837–41	President (Vice-President: Richard M. Johnson).
1840	Renominated, but defeated by Harrison.
1848	Unsuccessful Free-Soil candidate for President.
1862	Died: July 24, at Kinderhook, New York.

9.

WILLIAM HENRY HARRISON

1773–1841

1773	Born: February 9, in Berkeley, Virginia.
1791–96	Entered army after three years at Hampden-Sidney College. Campaigned in Indian fighting in the Northwest.
1795	Married: Anna Symmes (1775–1864).
1798	Secretary of the Northwest Territory.
1799–1801	Territorial Delegate in Congress.
1801–03	Governor of Indiana Territory.
1811	Defeated Tecumseh in the Battle of Tippecanoe.
1812–14	Major General of Kentucky Militia in War of 1812.
1816	Elected to Congress from Ohio.
1825	United States Senator.
1828	Minister to Colombia.
1841	President (Vice-President: John Tyler).
1841	Died in office: April 4, Washington, D.C.

10.

JOHN TYLER

1790–1862

1790	Born: March 29, in Greenway, Virginia.

1807	Graduated from College of William and Mary.
1813	Married: Letitia Christian (1790–1842), and Julia Gardiner (1820–1889) in 1844.
1816–21	Member of Congress.
1823–25	Member of Virginia Legislature.
1825	Elected Governor of Virginia.
1827–36	United States Senator.
1840	Elected Vice-President.
1841–45	President (Vice-President: none).
1844	Failed to be nominated for a Presidential term of his own.
1861	Elected to the Confederate Congress.
1862	Died: January 18, in Richmond, Virginia.

11.

JAMES KNOX POLK

1795–1849

1795	Born: November 2, near Little Sugar Creek, North Carolina.
1818	Graduated from University of North Carolina.
1820	Admitted to the bar, practiced law in Tennessee.
1821	Appointed Chief Clerk, Tennessee Senate.
1823	Member Tennessee Legislature.
1824	Married: Sarah Childress (1803–1891).
1825–39	Member United States Congress.
1839–41	Governor of Tennessee.
1845–49	President (Vice-President: George M. Dallas).
1849	Died: June 15, in Nashville, Tennessee.

12.

ZACHARY TAYLOR

1784–1850

1784	Born: November 24, in Orange County, Virginia.
1808	Appointed a Lieutenant in United States Army.
1810	Married: Margaret Smith (1788–1852). Promoted to Captain.
1812–15	Served in the War of 1812 against the British, fought Indians in Indiana, defended Fort Harrison.
1815–30	Assigned to various frontier Army posts. Acquired land and slaves in Mississippi and Louisiana.
1832–37	Appointed Colonel in Black Hawk War, and Brigadier General in Seminole War.
1840–46	Appointed to command the Department of the Southwest.
1846–47	Engaged in Mexican War at Palo Alto, etc., victor of the Battle of Buena Vista.
1849–50	President (Vice-President: Millard Fillmore).
1850	Died in office: July 9, in Washington, D.C.

13.

MILLARD FILLMORE

1800–1874

1800	Born: January 7, in Cayuga County, New York.
1819	Began to study law, while teaching school and working in a post office.
1823	Admitted to the bar. Began law practice in East Aurora, New York.
1826	Married: Abigail Powers (1798–1853).
1828	Elected to the New York Assembly.
1830	Moved to Buffalo, to prosperous law practice.
1833–45	Member of Congress.
1844	Defeated for the New York Governorship.
1847	Comptroller of New York State.
1849–50	Vice-President.
1850–53	President (Vice-President: none).
1856	Defeated for Presidency.
1858	Married Caroline Carmichael McIntosh (1813–1881).
1874	Died: March 8, at Buffalo, New York.

14.

FRANKLIN PIERCE

1804–1869

1804	Born: November 23, in Hillsboro, New Hampshire.
1824	Graduated from Bowdoin College.
1827	Admitted to the bar; began law practice in Hillsboro.
1829	Member New Hampshire Legislature.
1833	Elected to Congress.
1834	Married: Jane Means Appleton (1806–1863).
1837–42	United States Senator.
1846	Enlisted as a private in Mexican War.
1847–48	Became Colonel and Brigadier General, and injured in the Battle of Contreras. Resigned and returned to Concord, New Hampshire.
1853–57	President (Vice-President: William R. King).
1856	Defeated for renomination.
1869	Died: October 8, in Concord, New Hampshire.

15.

JAMES BUCHANAN

1791–1868

1791	Born: April 23, near Mercersburg, Pennsylvania
1809	Graduated from Dickinson College.
1812	Admitted to the bar.
1815	Member Pennsylvania State Legislature.
1820	Elected to Congress.
1831–33	Minister to Russia.

1834–45	United States Senator.
1853–56	Minister to Great Britain.
1857–61	President (Vice-President: John C. Breckinridge).
1868	Died: June 1, at Wheatland, near Lancaster, Pennsylvania.

16.

ABRAHAM LINCOLN

1809–1865

1809	Born: February 12, in Hardin County, Kentucky.
1816–30	Moved with parents to Indiana, grew up as a farm boy.
1831–37	Settled in New Salem, Illinois. Served briefly as Militia Captain in the Indian Black Hawk War. Failed as part-owner of a dry goods store. Appointed postmaster and land surveyor, studied law at night.
1834	Elected to the Illinois State Legislature.
1836	Admitted to the bar.
1837	Moved to Springfield, Illinois, and opened law office.
1842	Married: Mary Todd (1818–1882).
1847–49	Member of Congress.
1858	Lincoln-Douglas debate. Defeated for United States Senate.
1861–65	President (Vice-Presidents: Hannibal Hamlin, Andrew Johnson).
1861	Civil War began.
1865	Victory and assassination. Died: April 15, Washington, D.C.

17.

ANDREW JOHNSON

1808–1875

1808	Born: December 29, in Raleigh, North Carolina.
1826	Moved to Greenville, Tennessee, opened a tailor shop.
1827	Married: Eliza McCardle (1810–1876), who taught him to read and write.
1828	Alderman of Greenville.
1830	Mayor of Greenville.
1835	Member Tennessee State Legislature.
1841	State Senator.
1843	Member of Congress.
1853	Governor of Tennessee.
1857	United States Senator.
1862	Military Governor of Tennessee, with the rank of Brigadier General.
1865	Vice-President (March 4–April 15), succeeded to the Presidency when Lincoln was assassinated.
1865–69	President (Vice-President: none).
1868	Impeached, tried, and acquitted (by one vote).

1875	Elected to the United States Senate.
1875	Died: July 31, near Carter's Depot, Tennessee.

18.

ULYSSES S. GRANT

1822–1885

1822	Born: April 27, in Point Pleasant, Ohio.
1843	Graduated from West Point.
1846–47	Served with Generals Taylor and Scott in the Mexican War.
1848	Married: Julia Dent (1826–1902).
1854	Resigned from the Army.
1854–60	Lived in poverty, trying his luck as farmer, real estate dealer, clerk, etc.
1861–65	Appointed Colonel of Volunteers and promoted to General after successes in the field in the Civil War.
1865	Accepted Lee's surrender, as supreme Commander of the regular army.
1869–77	President (Vice-Presidents: Schuyler Colfax, Henry Wilson).
1885	Died: July 23, at Mount McGregor, New York.

19.

RUTHERFORD BIRCHARD HAYES

1822–1893

1822	Born: October 4, in Delaware, Ohio.
1842	Graduated from Kenyon College, Ohio.
1845	Admitted to the bar, after study at Harvard Law School.
1852	Married: Lucy Webb (1831–1889).
1858	Chosen City Solicitor of Cincinnati.
1861–65	Served in Civil War. Promoted to Brigadier General.
1865–67	Member of Congress.
1868–72	Governor of Ohio.
1872	Defeated for Congress.
1875	Reelected Governor for third term.
1877–81	President (Vice-President: William A. Wheeler).
1893	Died: January 17, at his Spiegel's Grove Estate, Fremont, Ohio.

20.

JAMES ABRAM GARFIELD

1831–1881

1831	Born: November 19, at Orange, Ohio.
1856	Graduated from Williams College.
1857–61	Instructor and Principal of Eclectic Institute of Hiram, Ohio.
1858	Became lay preacher in the Disciples of Christ Church.
1858	Married: Lucretia Rudolph (1832–1918).

1859	Ohio State Senator.
1860	Admitted to the bar.
1861	Commissioned Lieutenant Colonel, served in Civil War, became later a Major General.
1863–80	Member of Congress.
1880	Elected to the United States Senate.
1881	President (Vice-President: Chester A. Arthur).
1881	Shot by disappointed job-seeker, on July 2.
1881	Died: September 19, at Elberon, New Jersey.

21.

CHESTER ALAN ARTHUR

1830–1886

1830	Born: October 5, at Fairfield, Vermont.
1848	Graduated from Union College.
1854	After teaching school and private study, was admitted to the bar.
1859	Married: Ellen Lewis Herndon (1837–1880).
1861	Appointed Quartermaster General of New York State.
1863	Returned to law practice.
1871–78	Collector of the Port of New York.
1881	Vice-President (March 4–September 19).
1881–85	President (Vice-President: none).
1886	Died: November 18, at New York City.

22 and 24.

GROVER CLEVELAND

1837–1908

1837	Born: March 18, at Caldwell, New Jersey.
1855	After some interrupted schooling, became a student-clerk in a law office at Buffalo, New York.
1859	Admitted to the bar.
1863	Assistant District Attorney of Erie County, New York.
1871–73	Sheriff of Erie County.
1882	Mayor of Buffalo.
1883	Governor of New York State.
1885–89	President (Vice-President: Thomas A. Hendricks).
1886	Married: Frances Folsom (1864–1947).
1889	Returned to law practice in New York City.
1893–97	President (Vice-President: Adlai E. Stevenson).
1907	Retired to Princeton, New Jersey. Elected a Trustee of Princeton University.
1908	Died: June 24, at Princeton, New Jersey.

23.

BENJAMIN HARRISON

1833–1901

1833	Born: August 20, at North Bend, Ohio.
1852	Graduated from Miami University, Ohio.

1853	Married: Caroline Lavinia Scott (1832–1892).
1854	Admitted to the bar and practiced law in Cincinnati.
1860	Indiana State Supreme Court Reporter.
1862–65	Appointed Second Lieutenant of Indiana Volunteers. Served in the Civil War, became Captain, then Colonel and Brigadier General. Honorably discharged.
1876	Unsuccessful candidate for Governorship of Indiana.
1881	United States Senator.
1889–93	President (Vice-President: Levi P. Morton).
1893	Returned to law practice in Indianapolis.
1896	Married: Mary Scott Lord Dimmick (1858–1948).
1901	Died: March 13, at Indianapolis, Indiana.

25.

WILLIAM MCKINLEY

1843–1901

1843	Born: January 29, at Niles, Ohio.
1860	Attended Allegheny College in Pennsylvania.
1861	Enlisted as a volunteer in the Union Army.
1862–64	Promoted to Sergeant; became Second Lieutenant and Captain.
1865	Major of Volunteers.
1867	After reading law for two years, admitted to the bar.
1867–77	Practiced law in Canton, Ohio.
1871	Married: Ida Saxton (1847–1907).
1877–91	Member of Congress (with an interruption of one term).
1892	Governor of Ohio.
1897–1901	President (Vice-Presidents: Garret A. Hobart, Theodore Roosevelt).
1901	Shot by a young anarchist, at Buffalo's Pan-American Exposition, and died eight days later, on September 14, at Buffalo, New York.

26.

THEODORE ROOSEVELT

1858–1919

1858	Born: October 27, in New York City.
1880	Graduated from Harvard.
1880	Married: Alice Hathaway Lee (1861–1884).
1882	Member of New York State Assembly.
1884	Rancher in North Dakota.
1886	Married: Edith Kermit Carow (1861–1948).
1889	Appointed to the Civil Service Commission.
1895	President of New York City Police Board.
1897	Asssistant Secretary of the Navy.
1898	Colonel of Volunteer Cavalry (Rough Riders).

1898	Governor of New York.
1901	Vice-President (March 4–September 14).
1901–09	President (Vice-President: Charles W. Fairbanks).
1910	Big-game hunting expedition in Africa. Toured Europe.
1912	Defeated for the Presidency. Turned to writing.
1913	Explored jungles in Brazil.
1919	Died: January 6, at his home, Sagamore Hill, at Oyster Bay, New York.

27.

WILLIAM HOWARD TAFT

1857–1930

1857	Born: September 15, in Cincinnati, Ohio.
1878	Graduated from Yale University.
1880	Admitted to the bar, after graduating from Cincinnati Law School.
1881	Appointed Assistant Prosecuting Attorney.
1882	Collector of Internal Revenue.
1886	Married: Helen Herron (1861–1943).
1887	Judge, Ohio Superior Court.
1890	United States Solicitor General.
1892–1900	United States Circuit Court Judge.
1900	Commissioner and Governor General of the Philippines.
1904	Secretary of War.
1909–13	President (Vice-President: James S. Sherman).
1913–21	Professor of Law at Yale University.
1921–30	Chief Justice of the United States.
1930	Died: March 8, in Washington, D.C.

28.

WOODROW WILSON

1856–1924

1856	Born: December 28, at Staunton, Virginia.
1879	Graduated from Princeton University.
1882	After graduation from the University of Virginia Law School, admitted to the bar.
1882	Began practicing law at Atlanta, Georgia.
1885	Married: Ellen Louise Axson (1860–1914).
1886	Instructor of history and political economy at Bryn Mawr College.
1888	Taught history at Wesleyan University.
1890	Professor of jurisprudence and political economy at Princeton.
1902	President of Princeton University.
1911	Governor of New Jersey.
1913–21	President (Vice-President: Thomas R. Marshall).
1915	Married: Edith Bolling Galt (1872–1961).
1920	Awarded Nobel Peace Prize.
1924	Died: February 3, at Washington, D.C.

29.

WARREN GAMALIEL HARDING

1865–1923

1865	Born: November 2, at Corsica, Ohio.
1882	Attended Ohio Central College.
1884	Became editor and publisher of the Marion *Star*.
1891	Married: Florence Kling De Wolfe (1860–1924).
1898	Member Ohio State Senate.
1904	Lieutenant Governor of Ohio.
1910	Defeated for Governor.
1915	United States Senator.
1921–23	President (Vice-President: Calvin Coolidge).
1923	Died: August 2, at San Francisco, California.

30.

CALVIN COOLIDGE

1872–1933

1872	Born: July 4, at Plymouth, Vermont.
1895	Graduated from Amherst College.
1897	Admitted to the Massachusetts bar.
1900–04	City Solicitor and Clerk of Courts.
1905	Married: Grace Anne Goodhue (1897–1957).
1907–08	Member, Massachusetts Legislature.
1910–11	Mayor of Northampton.
1912–15	State Senator.
1916–18	Lieutenant Governor of Massachusetts.
1919–20	Governor.
1921–23	Vice-President.
1923–29	President (Vice-President: Charles G. Dawes).
1933	Died: January 5, at Northampton, Massachusetts. Buried: Plymouth, Vermont.

31.

HERBERT CLARK HOOVER

1874–1964

1874	Born: August 10, at West Branch, Iowa.
1895	Graduated from Stanford University.
1895–1914	Mining engineer.
1899	Married: Lou Henry (1875–1944).
1914–15	Chairman of American Relief Committee, London.
1915–19	Commissioner for Belgian Relief.
1917–19	United States Food Administrator.
1919–23	American Relief Administrator.
1921–28	Secretary of Commerce.
1929–33	President (Vice-President: Charles Curtis).
1964	Died: October 20, at New York City.

32.

FRANKLIN DELANO ROOSEVELT

1882–1945

1882	Born: January 30, at Hyde Park, New York.
1904	Graduated from Harvard University.
1905	Married: Anna Eleanor Roosevelt (1884–1962).
1907	Admitted to the bar, after Columbia Law School. Began law practice in New York City.
1910	Member State Senate.
1913	Assistant Secretary of the Navy.
1920	Defeated for Vice-President.
1921	Stricken with infantile paralysis.
1922–29	Practiced law in New York City.
1929	Governor of New York.
1933–45	President, for four terms (Vice-Presidents: John Garner, Henry Wallace, Harry S. Truman.)
1945	Died: April 12, at Warm Springs, Georgia.

33.

HARRY S. TRUMAN

1884–

1884	Born: May 8, at Lamar, Missouri.
1901	Graduated from high school. Went to work in various jobs: reporter on Kansas City *Star*, railroad timekeeper, bank clerk.
1906–17	Operated family farm in Independence, Missouri.
1917	Served in World War I, until the Armistice.
1919	Discharged as a Major. Operated, as partner, a haberdashery store in Kansas City, which failed.
1919	Married: Elizabeth (Bess) Virginia Wallace (1885–).
1922	Judge, Jackson County Court.
1925	Manager of a Building and Loan Company.
1926	Presiding Judge, Jackson County.
1935–45	United States Senator.
1945	Vice-President (January 20–April 12).
1945–53	President (Vice-President: Alben W. Barkley).

34.

DWIGHT D. EISENHOWER

1890–

1890	Born: October 14, in Denison, Texas.
1909	Graduated from high school in Abilene, Kansas.
1915	Graduated from West Point Military Academy.
1916	Married: Mamie Geneva Doud (1896–).
1918	Commanded tank training center at Camp Colt.
1919–29	In various military posts, advanced from Lieutenant to Major, to Colonel.

1935	Assistant to General MacArthur, Philippines.
1941	Brigadier General, with Chief of Staff, Third Army.
1942	Commander in Chief, Allied Forces in North Africa.
1943	Supreme Commander of Allied Expeditionary Force in Europe.
1944	General of the Army. Invaded Normandy.
1945	Chief of Staff, United States Army.
1948	President of Columbia University.
1950	Supreme Commander NATO Forces, Europe.
1953–61	President (Vice-President: Richard M. Nixon).
1961	Retired.

35.

JOHN F. KENNEDY

1917–1963

1917	Born: May 29, in Brookline, Massachusetts.
1940	Graduated from Harvard University. Wrote: *While England Slept*.
1941	Joined the U. S. Navy. Decorated for exploits in the Pacific.
1946	Elected to Congress, from Massachusetts.
1952	United States Senator.
1953	Married: Jacqueline Lee Bouvier (1929–).
1957	Won Pulitzer Prize for book *Profiles in Courage*.
1961–63	President (Vice-President: Lyndon B. Johnson).
1963	Assassinated in Dallas, Texas, November 22.

36.

LYNDON B. JOHNSON

1908–

1908	Born: August 27, near Stonewall, Texas.
1927	Entered Southwest Texas State Teachers College.
1930	Graduated from college and taught speech in Sam Houston High School.
1932	Secretary to Congressman Richard Kleeberg, in Washington.
1934	Married: Claudia Alta Taylor (1912–).
1937	Elected to Congress, reelected five times.
1941	Active war service as Naval Reserve officer.
1942	Left the service as Commander.
1949–61	United States Senator.
1955	Elected Majority Leader of the Senate.
1961–63	Vice-President.
1962	World tour.
1963	Succeeded to the Presidency on President Kennedy's death.
1964	Reelected President (Vice-President: Hubert H. Humphrey).

SOURCES
OF
PRESIDENTIAL
QUOTATIONS

*

GEORGE WASHINGTON

1. At Mount Vernon, to his friend Henry Knox, April, 1789.
2. Letter to his nephew, Bushrod Washington, January 15, 1783.
3. *Ibid.*
4. *Writings,* 1746.
5. April 19, 1785.
6. First Annual Message to Congress, January 8, 1790.
7. Farewell Address, September 19, 1796.
8. *Ibid.*
9. *Ibid.*
10. *Ibid.*

*

JOHN ADAMS

1. *The Adams Papers.*
2. Address to the citizens of Westmoreland, Virginia, July 11, 1789.
3. August, 1765.
4. To Thomas Jefferson, December 25, 1813.
5. *Ibid.,* June 20, 1815.
6. *Ibid.*
7. *Ibid.,* July 9, 1813.
8. *Works,* January 29, 1801.
9. To Secretary of State John Marshall, April 23, 1800.
10. *Works.*

*

THOMAS JEFFERSON

1. In Virginia, ca. 1774.
2. Letter to James Madison, January 30, 1787.
3. Original draft for the Declaration of Independence.
4. To Abbé Arnond, July 19, 1789.
5. Maryland, March 31, 1809.
6. *Writings,* Vol. VI (ca. 1802).
7. Letter to John Adams, 1815.
8. Letter to Du Pont de Nemours, April 24, 1816 (*Writings,* XIV).
9. To Dr. Benjamin Rush, September 23, 1800.
10. *Writings,* December 27, 1796.

*

JAMES MADISON

1. *National Gazette,* January 19, 1792.
2. *Ibid.*
3. *Tribune,* London, England.
4. Speech to Virginia Convention, December 2, 1829.
5. June 20, 1788.
6. *National Gazette,* February 2, 1792.
7. *Ibid.,* March 25, 1792.
8. February 2, 1792.
9. In 1816.
10. In 1788, *Federalist.*

*

JAMES MONROE

1. To F. A. Vanderkemp, January 24, 1818.
2. Message to Congress, May 4, 1822.
3. First Inaugural Address, March 4, 1817.
4. *Ibid.*
5. Seventh Annual Message to Congress, December 2, 1823.
6. *Ibid.*
7. First Inaugural Address, March 4, 1817.
8. Second Inaugural Address, March 5, 1821.
9. In 1793, to Thomas Jefferson.

*

JOHN QUINCY ADAMS
1. June 22, 1809.
2. Inauguration Address, March 4, 1825.
3. Speech, in 1821.
4. Speech, February 4, 1843.
5. In 1820, *Figures,* p. 66.
6. First Annual Message to Congress, December 6, 1825.
7. *Ibid.*
8. *Ibid.*
9. *Ibid.*
10. Diary, 1827.

*

ANDREW JACKSON
1. Second Inaugural Address, March 4, 1833.
2. Message to Congress, 1854.
3. *Life,* Parton.
4. *Quotations,* L. C. Henry.
5. 6th Annual Message to Congress, December 1, 1834.
6. *Messages and Papers,* July, 1832.
7. Veto Message, July 10, 1832.
8. Second Inaugural Address, March 4, 1933.
9. First Inaugural Address, March 4, 1829.
10. Quoted (from 1835) in *Decision-Making in the White House* by Theodore C. Sorensen.

*

MARTIN VAN BUREN
1. Inauguration Address, March 4, 1837.
2. *Ibid.*
3. First Annual Message to Congress, December 5, 1837.
4. From *Epoch,* 1826, p. 302.
5. Special Session Message, September 4, 1837.
6. Third Annual Message to Congress, December 2, 1839.
7. Third Annual Message to Congress, December 2, 1839.
8. Fourth Annual Message to Congress, December 5, 1840.
9. In *Autobiography,* 1854.

WILLIAM HENRY HARRISON

1. In 1812.
2. In Cincinnati, February, 1840.
3. During a Congressional debate, 1817.
4. "Log Cabin" campaign meeting, 1840.
5. On campaign tour, 1840.
6. *Ibid.*
7. *Ibid.*
8. Inauguration Address, March 4, 1841.

*

JOHN TYLER
1. *Champion,* June, 1855.
2. In 1816.
3. Protest to House of Representatives, August 30, 1842.
4. *Ibid.*
5. To Norwalk Democratic Association, September 2, 1844.
6. To 4th of July Committee, 1842.
7. *Ibid.*
8. *Diary,* in 1844.

*

JAMES KNOX POLK
1. *Diary,* December 2, 1848.

2. *Ibid.*, December 29, 1848.
3. *Ibid.*
4. *Diary*, January 25, 1847.
5. *Ibid.*
6. Inaugural Address, March 4, 1845.
7. *Ibid.*
8. *Ibid.*
9. *Diary*, March 1849.

*

ZACHARY TAYLOR
1. To J. S. Allison, April 12, 1848.
2. *Ibid.*
3. Inaugural Address, March 5, 1849.
4. *Old Rough and Ready*, by Silas Bent McKinley.
5. *Ibid.*
6. A statement of Taylor, to Hannibal Hamlin, July, 1850.
7. First Message to Congress, in 1849.
8. Quoted in *Old Rough and Ready*, by Silas Bent McKinley.
9. *Ibid.*

*

MILLARD FILLMORE
1. July 10, 1850.
2. To Daniel Webster (Fillmore's Secretary of State), October 28, 1850.
3. In 1856.
4. Speech at Newburgh, New York.
5. First Annual Message to Congress, December 2, 1852.
6. *Ibid.*
7. *Ibid.*
8. February, 1864.
9. Speech, June 26, 1856.
10. *Presidential Papers,* II, 139.

*

FRANKLIN PIERCE
1. Inaugural Address, March 4, 1853.
2. R. F. Nichols, *Franklin Pierce: Young Hickory of the Granite Hills.*
3. *Ibid.*
4. *Ibid.*
5. Inaugural Address, March 4, 1853.
6. Second Annual Message, December 4, 1854.
7. Letter, June, 1829.
8. Message to Congress, 1856.
9. Veto Message, May 3, 1854.

*

JAMES BUCHANAN
1. Speech, Greensburg, Pennsylvania, October 7, 1852.
2. Third Annual Message to Congress, December 19, 1859.
3. Inaugural Address, March 4, 1857.
4. Fourth Annual Message to Congress, December, 1860.
5. May 13, 1856.
6. Message to Congress, January 2, 1861.
7. Quoted in *The Presidents Speak* by Davis Newton Lott.
8. Message to Congress, February 2, 1858.
9. Speech at Wheatland, near Lancaster, Pennsylvania, March 6, 1861.

*

ABRAHAM LINCOLN
1. Speech at Springfield, Illinois, July 17, 1858.
2. Speech, Clinton, Illinois, September 2, 1858.

3. Speech, May 19, 1856.
4. Speech at Peoria, Illinois, October 16, 1854.
5. Speech, June 17, 1858.
6. Address at Gettysburg, November 19, 1863.
7. Second Inaugural Address, March 4, 1865.
8. Washington, D.C., 1864.
9. Letter to A. G. Hodges, April 4, 1864.
10. W. H. Lamon: *Recollections of Abraham Lincoln.*

*

ANDREW JOHNSON
1. St. Louis, Missouri, September 8, 1866.
2. Speech, New York, August, 1866.
3. First Annual Message to Congress, December 4, 1865.
4. Washington, D.C., February 22, 1866.
5. September, 1866.
6. Quoted in "Not Guilty," 1861, p. 54.
7. Speech, Nashville, Tennessee, 1864.
8. To Cabinet, November 30, 1867.
9. *Ibid.*
10. Speech, Washington, D.C., February 22, 1866.

*

ULYSSES S. GRANT
1. Letter, on acceptance of nomination, May 29, 1868.
2. From the illustrated autobiography, *Mr. Lincoln's General: U. S. Grant,* by Roy Meredith (ed.).
3. Memoirs, 1885.
4. Second Inaugural Address, March 4, 1873.
5. Message to Congress, December, 1876.
6. Annual Message to Congress, December 5, 1876.
7. A toast, in 1863.
8. Speech in Des Moines, Iowa, 1875.
9. According to the Rev. J. G. Cramer, in 1877, from *Meet General Grant,* by W. E. Woodward.
10. Quoted in *Presidential Wit,* by Bill Adler (ed.).

*

RUTHERFORD B. HAYES
1. Inaugural Address, March 4, 1877.
2. *Diary* of Rutherford Hayes, 1877.
3. *Ibid.,* p. 81.
4. *Ibid.,* p. 310.
5. *Ibid.,* p. 93.
6. *Ibid.,* p. 307.
7. *Ibid.,* p. 159.
8. *Ibid.,* March 1, 1878.
9. *Ibid.,* July 26, 1888.
10. *Ibid.,* December, 1891.

*

JAMES A. GARFIELD
1. To Whitelaw Reid, March 30, 1881.
2. W. R. Balch, *Maxims of James Abram Garfield,* p. 1.
3. *Ibid.*
4. *Journal,* June 8, 1881.
5. From a letter, April 21, 1880.
6. Letter, July 12, 1880.
7. Speech, Washington, D.C., June 29, 1869.
8. From *Maxims,* W. R. Balch, p. 23.
9. June 13, 1888.
10. *Facts,* p. 145.

*

CHESTER ALAN ARTHUR

1. Address, upon taking the oath of office, March 4, 1881.
2. *Ibid.*
3. Fourth Annual Message to Congress, December 1, 1884.
4. Veto Message, April 4, 1882.
5. *Ibid.*
6. 1878, *Arthur,* by F. G. Howe, p. 211.
7. *Ibid.*
8. Second Annual Message to Congress, December 4, 1882.
9. *Ibid.*
10. Veto Message to Congress, April 4, 1882.

*

GROVER CLEVELAND

1. *Grover Cleveland: the Man and the Statesman,* Vol. II, p. 321, by Robert McElroy (in 1904).
2. *Grover Cleveland: A Study in Courage,* by Allan Nevins.
3. In 1892, "Man & Statesman."
4. First Annual Message to Congresss, December 5, 1885.
5. First Inaugural Address, March 4, 1885.
6. Nevins: *Cleveland, op. cit.*
7. *Ibid.*
8. Second Inaugural Address, March 4, 1893.
9. *Ibid.*
10. Nevins: *Cleveland, op. cit.*

*

BENJAMIN HARRISON

1. In 1852.
2. In 1876, quoted in *Benjamin Harrison* by Harry Joseph Sievers.
3. First Inaugural Address, March 4, 1889.
4. In 1897.
5. March, 1901.
6. March 4, 1889.
7. Speech, 1888.
8. Inaugural Address, March 4, 1889.
9. *Ibid.*
10. Inscription on the Harrison statue, in Indianapolis.

*

WILLIAM MCKINLEY

1. Address, Pittsburgh, 1897.
2. Speech, Washington, D.C., 1890.
3. January 27, 1898, New York City.
4. September 8, 1900.
5. September 5, 1901.
6. *Ibid.*
7. S. C. Olcott: *Life of William McKinley.*
8. Speech, New York City, January 27, 1898.
9. Address at Cleveland, Ohio, July 4, 1894.
10. McKinley's last message, delivered at the Pan-American Exposition in Buffalo, September 5, 1901.

*

THEODORE ROOSEVELT

1. "Works" XIII, *The Adventure of Living* (July, 1918).
2. Speech, September 9, 1902, at Asheville, North Carolina.
3. Speech, 1908.
4. Speech at Minnesota State Fair, September 2, 1901.
5. *Autobiography,* 1911.
6. Speech at Cleveland, Ohio, November 5, 1910.
7. *Public Papers of F.D.R.* (Vol. 61).
8. From H. Pringle: *Theodore Roosevelt, a Biography.*
9. Inaugural Address, March 4, 1905.
10. Letter, September 10, 1909.

*

WILLIAM HOWARD TAFT

1. Chicago, Republican Convention, July 28, 1908.
2. *Taft,* by Alpheus Thomas Mason.
3. Speech, Boise, Idaho, November 3, 1906.
4. Speech in Tokyo, 1907.
5. Inauguration Address, March 4, 1909.
6. Address at Columbus, Mississippi, November 2, 1909.
7. Speech, 1920.
8. Quoted in *Taft and Roosevelt,* by A. Butt.
9. *Ibid.*
10. *Ibid.*

*

WOODROW WILSON

1. Speech at Des Moines, Iowa February 1, 1916.
2. Speech, 1916.
3. Address to Congress, April 2, 1917.
4. *Philosophy,* 1918, p. 39.
5. Speech, Richmond, Virginia, September 4, 1919.
6. Speech, Detroit, Michigan, July 10, 1916.
7. Speech, at West Point, New York, June 13, 1916.
8. Address to the Senate, January 22, 1917.
9. Address to the Senate, July 10, 1919.
10. Speech at Omaha, Nebraska, September 8, 1919.

*

WARREN G. HARDING

1. From *Autobiography* (1923).
2. Quoted in *Decision-Making in the White House,* by Theodore C. Sorensen.
3. Inaugural Address, March 4, 1921.
4. Address to Congress, April 12, 1921.
5. Second Annual Message to Congress, December 8, 1922.
6. Address to the Senate, February 10, 1922.
7. Speech at Marion, Ohio, October 1, 1920.
8. Speech, Boston, 1920.
9. Speech, July 9, 1923.
10. From *Masks in a Pageant,* by W. A. White.

*

CALVIN COOLIDGE

1. From *Meet Calvin Coolidge,* by E. C. Lathem (September 21, 1932).
2. Inaugural Address, March 4, 1925.
3. Speech, in New York City, February 12, 1924.
4. In 1925, Quoted in *Public Years,* by Bernard Baruch.
5. Address in Washington, D.C., January 17, 1924.
6. Inaugural Address, March 4, 1925.
7. *Public Years,* by Bernard Baruch (in 1925).
8. Speech to Associated Press, April 22, 1924.
9. Armistice Day Proclamation, October 21, 1919.
10. Speech, New York City, 1920.

*

HERBERT HOOVER

1. *American Quaker,* in 1917, p. 93.
2. Speech, November 15, 1929.
3. *Memoirs,* in 1931.
4. Armistice Day Address, 1929.
5. Report to Committee on Business Cycles, September 12, 1929.
6. Statement to the press, November 23, 1932.
7. Press Conference, October 17, 1930.
8. Speech to the Gridiron, December 14, 1929.
9. Detroit, October 22, 1932.
10. At the 1944 Republican Convention.

*

FRANKLIN D. ROOSEVELT
1. Acceptance of nomination for Presidency, Chicago, July 2, 1932.
2. Democratic Convention, Philadelphia, June 27, 1936.
3. First Inaugural Address, March 4, 1933.
4. Address, January 8, 1936.
5. Second Inaugural Address, January 20, 1941.
6. Fireside Chat, December 29, 1940.
7. Annual Message to Congress, January 6, 1941.
8. Campaign Address, Cleveland, Ohio, November 2, 1940.
9. Quoted in *Decision-Making in the White House,* by Theodore C. Sorensen.
10. *Ibid.*

*

HARRY S. TRUMAN
1. Inaugural Address, January 20, 1949.
2. Statement, White House, August 6, 1945.
3. To William Hillman in Washington, D.C., 1948.
4. *Ibid.*
5. Quoted in *Mr. President* (by William Hillman), in Washington, D.C., 1951.
6. *Ibid.,* 1948.
7. *Ibid.*
8. Interview, 1948.
9. *Ibid.,* 1950.
10. *Ibid.,* 1949.

*

DWIGHT D. EISENHOWER
1. Speech, June 23, 1945.
2. Farewell Address, January 17, 1961.
3. In the London *Sunday Times,* 1960.
4. Address, Ottawa, Canada, January 10, 1946.
5. Speech in Abilene, Kansas, June, 1945.
6. Speech, Columbia University, March 23, 1950.
7. Radio panel, June 3, 1963.
8. Press conference, April 30, 1958.
9. To the United Nations in New York, December 8, 1953.
10. Press conference, May 4, 1956.

*

JOHN F. KENNEDY
1. Press interview, 1962.
2. Acceptance of nomination for President, Los Angeles, California, July 15, 1960.
3. Quoted in *Saturday Review* of March 7, 1964 (in 1961).
4. Speech at Amherst College, October, 1963.
5. Inaugural Address, January 20, 1961.
6. *Ibid.*
7. *Ibid.*
8. *Ibid.*
9. Address to American University, Washington, D.C., June 10, 1963.
10. Address to the United Nations General Assembly, September 25, 1961.

*

LYNDON B. JOHNSON
1. Quoted, in 1963, from Isaiah 1 : 18.
2. Speech at New York Institute of Technology, December 16, 1958.
3. State of the Union Message, January 8, 1964.
4. Speech, Denver, Colorado, August 26, 1966.
5. State of the Union Message, January 8, 1964.
6. Speech on TV to the nation on civil disorders, July 27, 1967.
7. Address to Congress, November 27, 1963.
8. Nationwide television broadcast, March 31, 1968.
9. Address to the U.N. General Assembly hailing Nuclear Pact, June 12, 1968.
10. Television broadcast, March 31, 1968.

*

THE PARTY

We have a country as well as a party to obey.

—James Knox Polk

He serves his party best who serves his country best.

—Rutherford B. Hayes

I am afraid I am a constant disappointment to my party…
it seems to me to be impossible to be a strict party man
and serve the whole country impartially.

—William Howard Taft

What difference does party make when mankind is involved?

—Woodrow Wilson

THE PARTIES OF THE PRESIDENTS

1. George Washington	*Federalist*	
2. John Adams	*Federalist*	
3. Thomas Jefferson	*Republican*	
4. James Madison	*Republican*	
5. James Monroe	*Republican*	
6. John Quincy Adams	*Whig*	
7. Andrew Jackson	*Democratic*	
8. Martin Van Buren	*Democratic*	
9. William Henry Harrison	*Whig*	
10. John Tyler	*Whig*	
11. James K. Polk	*Democratic*	
12. Zachary Taylor	*Whig*	
13. Millard Fillmore	*Whig*	
14. Franklin Pierce	*Democratic*	
15. James Buchanan	*Democratic*	
16. Abraham Lincoln	*Republican*	
17. Andrew Johnson	*Democratic*	
18. Ulysses S. Grant	*Republican*	
19. Rutherford B. Hayes	*Republican*	
20. James A. Garfield	*Republican*	
21. Chester A. Arthur	*Republican*	
22-24. Grover Cleveland	*Democratic*	
23. Benjamin Harrison	*Republican*	
25. William McKinley	*Republican*	
26. Theodore Roosevelt	*Republican*	
27. William Howard Taft	*Republican*	
28. Woodrow Wilson	*Democratic*	
29. Warren G. Harding	*Republican*	
30. Calvin Coolidge	*Republican*	
31. Herbert Hoover	*Republican*	
32. Franklin D. Roosevelt	*Democratic*	
33. Harry S. Truman	*Democratic*	
34. Dwight D. Eisenhower	*Republican*	
35. John F. Kennedy	*Democratic*	
36. Lyndon B. Johnson	*Democratic*	

ACKNOWLEDGMENTS

My sincere thanks to friends who looked and listened; to the authors of scholarly works, from whose diligence I borrowed (and credited where I could, in the "Sources") ; to the friendly staffs of The New-York Historical Society and The New York Public Library, for their kind assistance in my search for documentation; and to the painters and photographers whose works, most of bygone days, inspired my images. My sincere thanks are due, too, to the last seven American Presidents I was privileged to draw from life, and on which drawings I based the last seven of these present calligraphic renderings of my Presidential likenesses. And last but not least, thanks to the Publishers who followed my suggestions in their lavish production of the book—and to Ann, my wife, who patiently suffered my changes of mood while *The Presidents* was born.